450
Low-Cost
No-Cost
Strategies
for recognizing,
rewarding & retaining
good people

Volume II

By: Carol A. Hacker

Carol A. Hacker & Associates
209 Cutty Sark Way
Alpharetta, Georgia 30005
PHONE - 770-410-0517
FAX - 770-667-9801

www.carolahacker.com
Carol@CarolAHacker.com

Carol A. Hacker & Associates, ©2004

ISBN 0-9662011-2-4

This publication is designed to provide accurate and authoritative information in regards to the subject matter covered. It is sold with the understanding that neither the author nor the publisher is engaged in rendering legal, accounting, or other professional service. If legal advice or other expert assistance is required, the services of a competent professional should be sought.

From a Declaration of Principles jointly adopted by a Committee of the American Bar Association and a Committee of Publishers.

Printed in the United States of America.

Contents

Acknowledgments

Thanks are in order to everyone who contributed to the ideas found in this book. Many of you were in my seminars over the past several years. Other suggestions came from friends and clients—people who are currently implementing creative ways to show appreciation for their employees and have fun at the same time. All of you are making a difference on a day-to-day basis. Keep it up!

Special thanks to Jeanne Sharbuno—speaker, career coach, author, and editor. You've done a wonderful job in helping me with this book. I've said it before and I'll say it again, if I could have a sister, I would choose you. Thanks for being such a special friend. We're connected by our roots in Wisconsin; by chance we met in Atlanta—for that I feel truly blessed.

Bill and Cher Holton—you continue to inspire me with your energy and extraordinary talent. I think back to January 1989 when I was getting started in business and we met. I knew then that we would someday become good friends. Little did I know that you would be the inspiration and driving force behind my success as a speaker and writer. Here's to many more Margaritavilles!

Bill Coffman—my dear friend. You are one of the most creative people I know. Lucky the people who get to work for you! You set the example in leading your team. Thanks for generously sharing some of the wonderful things you do with and for your employees. You continue to set the example in going above and beyond.

Woody McKay—you will always be in a class by yourself! Your sense of humor and wit are second to none. I've learned so much from you about writing and life over the years that we've been friends. Thanks for your contributions to this book and for being such a good friend to me.

Thanks to all of the contributors to this book, both known and unknown to me. Suggestions have come from sources of all kinds. Even the stranger on the airplane that shared his best idea for recognizing his employees is appreciated. I couldn't have done it without help from all of you.

About the Author

Carol A. Hacker is an educator, speaker, and the founder of Carol A. Hacker & Associates, one of the country's foremost skill-building enterprises for human resource management. For more than two decades, she's been a significant voice in front-line and corporate human resource management to Fortune 100 companies as well as small businesses. She ranks among the experts in the field of recruiting and retention issues. With hands-on experience in managing a wide variety of public, private, and non-profit consulting and training projects, her client list spans North America and Europe.

Prior to starting her own firm in January 1989, Carol held a number of management positions including that of Director of Human Resources for the North American Division of Bahlsen Inc., a multi-million dollar European manufacturer.

Carol is the author of eleven business books and over 150 published articles. (See pages 49 and 50 of this book for more information on her books and CDs). Her first book, *Hiring Top Performers-350 Great Interview Questions For People Who Need People,* is a bestseller and great resource for people who are responsible for hiring others.

She is a member of the National Speakers Association and speaks to professional and trade associations, as well as to private corporations and government agencies. She draws on her strong business background to tailor management training programs for organizations of all sizes. Her motivational presentations are practical, positive, and entertaining. Her interactive workshops have helped thousands of managers become better leaders. Carol earned her B.S. and M.S. with honors from the University of Wisconsin.

Some of her most popular workshops include:

◆ How to Hire Top Performers
◆ How to Take the Guesswork Out of Interviewing
◆ How to Build a Retention Culture
◆ How to Keep the People Who Keep You in Business
◆ Leadership in a Changing Environment
◆ How to Conduct "Win-Win" Performance Appraisals
◆ Leading a Team in a Changing Environment
◆ How to Give Critical Feedback Without Causing Defensiveness
◆ Enhancing Working Relationships

Introduction

The tremendous success of the first volume of this book has resulted in the creation of *450 Low-Cost/No-Cost Strategies for recognizing, rewarding & retaining good people-Volume II.* It's about recognition, rewards, and what it takes to retain good people. Exceptional organizations find a way to do this; they understand that recognition penetrates where money can't. You may have to make a financial investment; however, more often than not, more time than cash is required. Yes, time is money, but you can't expect to run a business without spending *some* money. And what better place to spend a bit of your organization's hard-earned profits than on the employees who made it possible? Keep in mind that "low-cost/no-cost" means different things to different people. What may seem like a lot of money to you may not be to another organization. Work within your budget and have fun!

In July 2001 WorldatWork (formerly the American Compensation Association and the Canadian Compensation Association) and the National Association for Employee Recognition (NAER) conducted a joint survey. They surveyed 539 companies and found that 86 percent have a recognition program and that 62 percent of those that do not are thinking about creating one. Now this doesn't mean that those who don't have a formal recognition program never recognize or reward their employees. They just don't have a program plan in place that they follow.

The results of this above-mentioned survey yielded the following information regarding the most common ways employees are recognized.

- Presentation of recognition awards at one-on-one meetings with managers (71 percent).
- Special events like banquets or luncheons (65 percent).
- Staff meetings (60 percent).
- Company-wide meetings (42 percent).

However, let's go beyond this survey, and on with this book. Herein are hundreds of ideas from the practical to the zany that have been shared by managers, supervisors, business owners, and rank and file employees.

Use these ideas to challenge your own creative senses as well as those of your employees. Get your employees involved and find out how they want to be recognized for going the extra mile as well as for simple, daily achievements. Don't assume that incentives which get the "Boomers" and "Geezers" fired up will get your "Generation X and Y" employees excited. Most likely totally different things turn them on.

Rosabeth Moss Kanter accurately summed up the idea of employee reward, recognition, and retention with the following: "Compensation is a right, recognition is a gift." William Makepeace Thackeray added his thoughts: "Next to excellence is the appreciation of it."

5

Chapter 1 - Recognition

"Recognition is the most powerful strategy your company can give your employees to achieve better business results and retain your best people."

—From the book, *Managing With Carrots*
by Adrian Gostick and Chester Elton

Everyone wins when you consistently praise and recognize your employees—not just during annual performance reviews. Rewards, incentives, and positive feedback are like carrots; they're there to get people motivated and on task. Most people like to know that their time and efforts are being noticed and appreciated. A simple word of "thanks," a surprise lunch for a good job, or special treats for an employee's birthday can go a long way. Simple things that don't require much time can brighten up an employee's day—much more than a manager can begin to imagine. Take time to acknowledge your employees for their many accomplishments both large and small. Let them know they're valued. Here are some ideas to get you started:

1.   Recognize employees for a special accomplishment with a two-dollar bill.

2.   Send "welcome aboard" cards to all new-hires.

3.   Send a letter to the employee's family praising his or her accomplishments.

4.   Hold a voluntary "good news spot" once a week for 15 minutes. Everyone shares one good thing that's happened in his or her life at work in the past 5 days.

5.   Celebrate *everything* you can—exceeding goals, meeting an exceptional challenge, attaining a good safety record, improving customer relations, eliminating waste, managing costs, signing a big contract, improving efficiencies, or any other employee achievements or heroics.

6.   Hold a "Thank a Customer Party." Everyone invites a customer and presents him or her with a certificate of appreciation.

7.   Create recognition programs that might revolve around any of the following: Cleanest work area, most consistent on-time record, exceptional customer service, meeting or exceeding goals, best overall new idea, most creative cost-saving idea, best safety record, fewest absences, or completion of a special assignment.

8.   If your company deserves recognition for its employee-friendly policies, get it placed on a *Best Place to Work* list such as that published in *Working Mother* and *Business Week* magazines.

Recognition continued...

9. Invite spouses and significant others to attend company meetings where everyone can ask questions of top management.

10. Have business cards waiting for new-hires when they show up for their first day of work.

11. Recognize diversity and the importance of working with people of all kinds. Face your own prejudices. How you treat people who are "different" speaks volumes about who you are as a person.

12. Read letters from satisfied customers at staff meetings, then post them on company bulletin boards.

13. One division of a company purchased a gong on E-Bay. Individual and team achievements are celebrated with the sound of the gong.

14. After employees retire, rehire them part-time in the same or different job. Allow them a flexible work schedule. It's better than losing them altogether because they no longer want to work full time.

15. Design a "Go-Getter Wall" where employees' accomplishments are recognized. Postings can range from customer appreciation letters to achievements and milestones for individuals and teams.

16. Print on the back of every paycheck the words: "The company is doing well because of your hard work. Thank you."

17. When someone leaves your organization, don't ignore the fact that the loss of an employee puts a burden on your other employees. Anticipate the fact that your existing employees will be willing and able to pick up the slack only so long before they become frustrated; you then run the risk of losing them too. Show appreciation for the fact that they are holding things together until you can hire someone to replace the person(s) that left.

18. Recognize employees with stickers and pins that they can wear on hardhats and caps. You might even consider recognizing top performers with a special hat.

19. Try "pats on the back" to recognize your employees as does a hotel in Tomah, Wisconsin. Guests of the hotel have the opportunity to complete a "pat on the back" card complimenting an employee. The hotel manager takes the two employees with the most compliments each month out to lunch.

20. Lead the team of employees in a standing ovation for an employee(s) that has done an exceptional job.

Recognition continued...

21. At the time a job offer is made and accepted, tell the new-hire that dinner for two is compliments of the company to celebrate the new job. This takes place *before* the new employee joins the company; it's a great way to say, "welcome."

22. Send a fruit basket to the home of your new employee with a "welcome aboard" note.

23. Publish and post the "wins" in your department or company.

24. Rather than spend money on expensive artwork for your hallways, showcase photos of your employees at work and play.

25. Construct a brick or concrete walkway on company property where each employee has his or her name inscribed. Update it as more people are hired and stay with you for a specific period of time.

26. Pay for a sitting fee and color portrait in honor of births, marriages, and milestone wedding anniversaries.

27. Recognize an employee's aptitude or skill by inviting him or her to teach or coach others in a technique.

28. At a high tech company, the human resources manager started a "Warm Fuzzy" recognition program. Employees nominate each other to receive an over-sized fuzzy-faced stick-on. Employees put them up in their cubicles and when job applicants tour the company, they're always interested in how, why, and where the warm fuzzies come from. People are proud to tell them it's just a fun and simple way employees are recognized for their efforts.

29. Say thanks with a unique gift of chocolate from Totally Chocolate. Choose from embossed candy bars that say" "thank you," "think safety," "we can't spell success without u," "thanks a million," "happy birthday," "welcome," (for new-hires) and more. Contact their web site at: www.totallychocolate.com or call: 1-800-255-5506.

30. Hold weekly ten-minute "vision meetings." Ask everyone to share what he or she did that week that brought them closer to meeting the organization's vision.

31. Allow your employees to participate in scheduling their work. This is especially successful with hourly employees. Get them involved in designing a work schedule that is viewed as fair to everyone. Increase commitment by getting their "buy-in."

32. Recognize your employees' anniversary with the company as well as employees' birthdays on your company web site.

Recognition continued...

33. The canopy over the employee entrance at a hotel reads: "V.I.P. ENTRANCE." The sign next to the door says: "Through this door pass the most dedicated hotel employees in town. You *are* the best. Thank you for being here!"

34. Award your employees with two movie passes on their birthday.

35. Acknowledge customer praise of your employees by posting and/or reading letters of thanks from customers.

36. In the hospitality industry, recognize employees with a cash bonus if a shift does an exceptionally good job when short-staffed. It's a great way to keep up good morale.

37. Send a birthday card singing telegram on the employee's birthday that's delivered by the supervisor or manager or even the entire team.

38. Give every employee a candy cane during the December holidays with a "thank you" ribbon tied to it.

39. Keep a supply of note cards on your desk. At the end of the day, take a few minutes to write thank you notes to deserving employees.

40. Present your employees with a plate of cookies and chocolates or anything appropriate with a card that says: "Thanks for all of your hard work!"

41. Recognize all of your employees for small improvements. Recognition is not just about saluting your superstars.

42. The more personal the recognition, the more meaningful it is. Find a way to make every recognition event personal. Maybe it's as simple and cost-effective as handwriting a note to your employees thanking them for their contributions.

43. Invite employees that ordinarily wouldn't have the opportunity to interface with customers to have lunch or dinner with them.

44. Take the time to tell a colleague or manager from another department about the good work that one of their employees did while supporting you and/or your team.

45. Dedicate a song to your employees on the radio. Make sure they hear it.

46. Have a complete meal delivered to an employee (at home) who has worked overtime and won't have time to cook dinner. Take turns surprising different employees as a way of thanking them for their extra efforts.

47. Provide noisemakers, confetti, and party hats to help your team applaud their success.

Recognition continued...

48.   Get to work before everyone else so that your can greet your employees personally and offer them a cup of coffee, tea or soft drink.

49.   Be visible—and not just when you need someone to do something. Get out of your office and talk to your people. This is just as true for the frontline supervisor as it is for the VPs and President of the company. And for the executives, don't limit yourself to the high profile areas. Get out and see your people in the operational trenches (customer service, order entry, claims, the shop floor—anywhere where there's hands on processing). Let people know they are appreciated and that they make a difference.

50.   Recognize and reward employees who work on non-scheduled days. These are the people you call on to work on weekends, holidays and/or their day(s) off. We often take these people and their loyalty for granted. Treat them special. Don't ask the same people to make this kind of sacrifice all of the time or you run the risk of losing them, especially if you fail to recognize and thank them.

51.   Break out the chalk and write a message of appreciation to your employees on the shop floor or walk way to the entrance of the building in which they work.

52.   If they miss a sale or a deal falls apart, it doesn't make them a bad person, it doesn't make them a failure. Expect and reward success, but accept human limitations and bad luck.

53.   At the beginning of the day, put five coins in your pocket. Then, during the day, each time you recognize an employee for an accomplishment, transfer a coin to your other pocket.

54.   Write a note of thanks on the back of your business card and hand it to an unsuspecting employee in a gesture of appreciation.

55.   Invite employees to a ten-minute "stand-up" meeting whereby everyone gets positive feedback from his or her manager. Do this periodically; if done too often it loses its value.

56.   Implement a "Catch Employees Doing Something Right" program.

57.   Be your own cheerleader. Set the example. If you're having a bad day, get over it. Your attitude is contagious; your employees will model what you do and feel.

58.   Personally hand out gift certificates or cash bonuses so that you can add your verbal "thank you" to your congratulations.

Recognition continued...

59. Personally thank your employees for doing a good job. Be specific about what they did that made a difference. Then put your praise in writing. Copy other members of management if appropriate.

60. For employees who complete a particularly difficult training class, recognize them with a $100 bill.

61. Consider an *Employee Recognition Program* to provide an opportunity for all employees to nominate deserving staff for their outstanding achievements. It's a way to thank those individuals who go above and beyond in carrying out their responsibilities and who put the needs of others above their own. While the tradition of success is directly attributable to team effort, it is the individual who contributes the knowledge, professionalism, dedication, and productivity that allows the organization as a whole to present to their customers a high standard of product and/or services. This program allows all employees to recognize individuals, grouped according to their functional area, quarterly on a statewide basis, and annually on both a regional and national basis.

62. Cut the number of pay grades and broaden them to allow more latitude in raises. It's one of the best ways to recognize good performance.

63. Give pay raises every 90 days. The raises should correspond with the acquisition of new skills.

64. Hold a "People Make a Difference Week." Kickoff the event with breakfast with the company's president and all employees.

65. Select a performance goal that you would like to recognize for the month such as highest customer satisfaction rating. Employees vote for the winner. The winner gets the use of a very special chair for the month. One company calls it their "musical chair."

66. Supervisors recognize their employees with a "Moment of Truth" award in the weekly staff meeting at one company. The honored employee is awarded a gift certificate from Home Depot or a local department store.

67. Make employees a part of your weekly "to do" list. Add the names of the people who report to you to your list of goals to accomplish. Then cross off names as you recognize them with positive feedback.

68. If recognizing employees is hard for you, delegate the task to an employee who enjoys and is good at making people feel good. Make employee recognition a formal part of his or her job description.

11

Chapter 2 - Awards/Rewards

*"If you don't reward your key people,
the competition will."*

—Bill Grace as quoted in
Restaurant Business Magazine

"Key people" refers to ALL of your employees rather than only a select few. There's much wisdom in the words above that are important for managers and business owners to remember. People will leave if they feel taken advantage of or are not acknowledged for their efforts. Awards and rewards can head-off turnover and low-morale at the pass.

An <u>award</u> is something that is bestowed for performance and achievement. Awards can be large or small. Large awards usually happen once a year, whereas small awards are presented throughout the year. An award is generally presented when an employee achieves a goal, wins a contest, or is part of a team that reaches a major benchmark.

A <u>reward</u> is something given as recognition for worthy actions and behavior. Rewards have to do with efforts rather than achievements. They are more emotional than tangible. They're more materially significant. They may influence performance significantly because people want to earn the prize, even if small. Give rewards as a motivation for employees to meet specific expectations. Or use rewards as recognition for striving for excellence. Some examples might include rewarding people for going beyond the call of duty on a demanding project or when they're asked to give up a Saturday to be at work.

Awards and rewards can either be planned or spontaneous. Planned awards/ rewards are something employees know about ahead of time, which gives them something to work towards, whereas spontaneous awards/rewards come as a surprise. Whichever the case, remember to acknowledge your employees throughout the year for their outstanding performance and efforts—both large and small.

1.   Let your employees give co-workers a day off with pay. Put a specific number of days in a "bank" and allow employees to recognize their peers with time off. However, this needs a formal plan so that everyone understands how this works.

2.   Pay for the college tuition or a portion thereof, for children of employees whose parents have worked for the company 5 years or more.

3.   Create an "overdo for a reward" list. Work to reward employees on the list who deserved to be recognized for their achievements.

12

Awards/Rewards continued...

4. Offer a grab bag of privileges such as leave two hours early, arrive two hours late, schedule own time for a week, pick a job for a day, take a day off with pay, free parking for a week in the president's space, or any other privilege offered for a short period of time.

5. At the end of the probationary period of 3 months or 6 months, present your new employee with a small gift. Company identified merchandise such as a cap, mug, T-shirt are often popular items.

6. Give your employees an opportunity to "buy" additional vacation time. Days are "sold" in 1/2 day increments at any price you determine to be fair.

7. For employees that are required to travel, provide them with a web cam so that they can check in on their families and pets when they're away from home.

8. As a reward for employees that are adventurous, send them to Skydive University in Sebastian, Florida, 80 miles South of Orlando. They offer instruction for all levels of ability. It's the perfect environment for jumping with views of the Kennedy Space Center, sunsets over Lake Okeechobee, and proximity to the turquoise waters of the Sebastian Inlet. Contact them at: www.skydiveu.com or 1-800-891-JUMP.

9. One company has a "mistake of the month" club. An award is given for trying new things, even if it doesn't work. The goal is to create an environment where people are willing to take calculated risks. In this instance, the manager won for the first two months to help people get over the fear of being recognized for making a mistake.

10. Offer referral bonuses and hold monthly drawings for a bottle of Dom Perignon®, airline tickets, Palm Pilots®, laptop computers, gift certificates, and flowers. When an employee refers someone that's hired, they become eligible for quarterly drawings for even larger prizes.

11. Close the office at noon on holiday weekends and/or Fridays.

12. Offer your employees generous amounts of time off once their jobs are complete. Example: As soon as they hit their monthly goals, they can go home every afternoon at 2 p.m. for the rest of that month. In addition, the first salesperson to meet his or her target gets the last two days of the month off with pay.

13. Give every employee that graduates from high school/college a cash bonus.

14. Send free baby formula in installments to new parents for the baby's first year of life.

13

Awards/Rewards continued...

15. Implement more frequent salary reviews than you currently have. Many companies are using this strategy as a way to let their employees know they are valued.

16. At one company, employees are given P.T.O. (paid time off). Vacation and sick leave days get lumped together. Employees earn the P.T.O. and then take the time off when they want to. They are required to take a minimum of 10 days off every year. The company will buy back P.T.O. if employees prefer the cash.

17. Give newlywed employees one extra week of paid vacation.

18. Pick a first name out of a hat once a month. Everyone with that first name is treated to an extra 15 minutes for lunch for one day.

19. When an employee is sent out of town on business at the end of the week, as a reward for exceeding expectations, pay the expenses (hotel and meals) for the employee to stay up to three additional days; it's a mini-vacation.

20. Hire employees' children before you hire outsiders to fill in for summer vacations or holidays.

21. A company hires college interns for the summer. If the supervisor trains the intern well enough, he or she can take the summer off without pay. In one instance, the supervisor who had small children had three consecutive months off. That benefit prevented that employee from resigning because she could be at home with her young children during the summer. It was a win-win situation.

22. Consider a "980" work schedule that enables employees to have a three day weekend every other week. Monday through Thursday of Week One, employees will work nine-hour days; and on Friday, they'll work eight hours. During Week Two, they'll work nine hours Monday through Thursday and have Friday off.

23. Once a year, give every employee $100 and take them to a shopping center or mall with instructions that they *must* spend the money on *themselves*.

24. Give your employee a personal assistant for a day.

25. Between the months of April and September, (the company's slow season), employees may take off one-half day cach month with pay. If they choose to take off an additional half-day, they are allowed to make up the time as long as it's completed within the two-week pay period.

26. Pay for tutoring for an employee's school-age child or children up to a limited dollar amount annually.

Awards/Rewards continued…

27. If you can't give employees a day off with pay, reward them with a "bonus hour" off with pay in the middle of the day. Let them accumulate up to four hours that they may take with their supervisor's approval.

28. Offer "the broken arm" award to employees who "broke their arm" pushing to get the job done. A miniature plastic arm in a sling is what one company used for recognition.

29. Provide "funny money" that supervisors can give to their employees. Twenty "funny money" dollars can buy a gift certificate to a department, music, or grocery store.

30. Award the *Employee of the Month* with a luncheon for which he or she may invite three guests.

31. Offer paid sabbaticals to employees with three years of tenure.

32. In the hotel industry, housekeepers who get high scores for cleaning rooms are rewarded with "ownership" of a block of rooms as a permanent responsibility.

33. Surprise your employees with a bonus check. If they put the check into their 401K plan, the company matches the amount with 50 cents on the dollar.

34. Award "Bug Bucks" as is done by one high-tech company to employees who identify and propose a solution for a technical problem outside their area of responsibility. "Bug Bucks" can be exchanged for gift items at the end of each quarter.

35. A hospital offers a "Thumbs Up" award that employees can give one another or supervisors and patients can award to employees. "Thumbs Up" is simply a sticker of a thumb pointing up. It has become extremely coveted as employees apply the stickers to their name badges. Employees and supervisors submit nominations via e-mail with a brief description of why the award is deserved. Patients can also give deserving employees a pre-printed "Thumbs Up" card that the employee turns in for points that can be used for gifts offered in a gift catalogue.

36. Start a "100 Club." "100" stands for the number of points an employee must have to become a member of the Club. They earn points for attendance, punctuality, no lost time accidents, achieving production goals, and accuracy. Once a Club member, employees can earn and redeem points for gift items.

37. Award a U.S. Savings Bond upon the birth of the employee's child.

38. Award employees who have perfect attendance for the year with a day off with pay.

15

Awards/Rewards continued...

39.   When honored with a major quality award by an industry group, make plans to share the recognition with the employees who made it all happen. Award each employee a commemorative gift. If you're not sure what to give, ask your employees to make suggestions.

40.   One company designed a "Gotch Ya" award. All employees received a supply of $1 gift certificates to local stores. They were asked to award them to deserving co-workers in recognition for good work.

41.   Give your employees a chance to earn a free car detailing. This could be done in the form of a simple contest.

42.   Distribute one quarter (or a certain percentage) of the company's profits among your employees every quarter.

43.   Give "Super Server Awards" to the people that best exemplify superb service to your customers. Co-workers determine who receives the awards.

44.   When employees pass 10 years with the company, send them on a trip for two anywhere in the country (or world) with all expenses paid up to a certain amount.

45.   Reward a bonus to employees who stay with you for a specified period of time.

46.   Highlight success. Use flipchart paper to set up an employee graffiti wall depicting daily or weekly accomplishments. Don't forget to include your own.

47.   Offer a "support from home" option which allows support staff to work from home at least part of the time.

48.   If you award a bonus, send a handwritten note along with cash or a check.

49.   In a retail store, employees who work past December 25th receive a bonus in the form of a gift card that can be used on the retailer's web site or at any of its stores.

50.   Give your employees 25% of their annual salary in one lump sum at the *beginning* of the year. It's not a bonus, but regular, anticipated earnings paid in advance.

51.   Reward employees with one year's worth of selections from a book club.

52.   Don't forget your volunteers. Reward and recognize them every quarter with a special gift or gift certificate.

53.   After a particularly tough week, treat your team to bagels/donuts and coffee.

16

54. Have your *Employees of the Month* vote for an *Employee of the Year*. Invite all 12 winners to a special luncheon or dinner. At the end of the meal, hold a drawing for a grand prize trip for two or a number of smaller prizes.

55. For animal lovers—let employees earn a gift certificate to Animalden's on-line store. Contact them at: www.animalden.com.

56. The employee with the most customer compliments in a month wins dinner for two or a cash award. Post a sheet with employees' names, what customers said and the tally of compliments for the month.

57. Give your team of employees a chance to earn a $250 shopping spree at the store of their choice. Each team member gets a gift certificateAt a brake parts store, delivery drivers are awarded $100 in cash if they don't have an accident with the company vehicle for 6 months.

58. Reward deserving employees with 4 hours of pampering at a Day Spa.

59. Award your employees who meet specific goals or deadlines a specific amount of Internet 'play" time. Provide a selection of games.

60. Surprise your employees with a 5-pound box of Godiva® Chocolates when they exceed their goals for the month or quarter.

61. A sandwich shop awards its drivers $75 in cash for every three months they are not absent from work or late to work more than once.

62. Hold a "roll-out-of-bed" breakfast picnic on company property for employees who have to work on Saturday or Sunday.

63. Reward employees with custom prepaid long distance phone cards. Design your own or let a professional graphics design team create your card. For more information, check this out: info@customphonecard.com.

64. Like the military, give out a 3-day pass to deserving employees. Don't charge them vacation or personal time—this is a reward for *exceptional* performance.

65. Surprise your Call Center employee and take over answering his or her phone for an hour or two while the employee relaxes or takes a long lunch.

66. Consider a *Chairman's Award* that is given each year to deserving staff for their extraordinary contribution. It is presented to an individual or team whose accomplishments best reflect commitment to the organization's core values.

Awards/Rewards continued…

67. Reward employees with additional time off when they finish their assignments before the deadline. Do so with the understanding that sloppy work is unacceptable and does not count toward extra time off.

68. Present a "Million Dollar" candy bar to employees with an exceptional idea.

69. Call Center employees came up with a crazy traveling trophy that is awarded at the end of each week to the team with the funniest phone call of the week.

70. When a company reaches a financial milestone, reward your employees with stock.

71. If you are a retail employer, trade gift certificates with other local merchants. Use the gift certificates to reward your team members.

72. Award your employees a day off with pay if they work for 6 months without a personal injury accident.

73. The prize for a special contest at one company is a dinner party for the winner and guests at the president's home where he and his wife act as hosts. The candlelight meal is prepared and served; transportation by limousine is provided for everyone.

74. As an alternative to traditional service awards, present your employees with their choice of a signed and numbered limited edition print or photograph.

75. Host a Pumpkin & Chili Party. This festive event features pig races, a corn maze, comedy and juggling show, entertainment, carousel rides, a pumpkin patch, chili dinner with roasted sweet corn, bonfires and marshmallow roasting.

76. In special recognition of an employee, for a contribution of $25 or more, Trees Atlanta will plant a shade tree in honor of anyone you name. The recipient will receive a holiday tree greeting card announcing your gift. Contact Trees Atlanta at: 404-522-4097 or visit their web site at: www.treesatlanta.org.

77. A "Shining STAR" employee recognition program was put in place in order to recognize and reward employees in one company who consistently go the extra mile to provide professional, quality customer service. The focus of the program is the S.T.A.R. Standards of Excellence—Service, Teamwork, Attitude and Respect. Recognition goes to employees who distinguish themselves by their exemplary performance in these areas.

Chapter 3 - Camaraderie

"Celebration is more than a happy feeling.
Celebration is an experience. It is like helping others,
accepting others, laughing with others."

—Douglas R. Stuva

A winning workplace is one where employees and managers get to know each other and come to care about and respect each other—not just as co-workers but as individuals too. Camaraderie creates a more personal and enjoyable atmosphere, which in turn fosters increased productivity and improved employee retention. There's something about shared fun, food, and brainstorming that motivates a team to perform better.

Developing camaraderie may take place after hours or during the workday. Remember not to let the small "cost" of your employees' time away from their work stop you from scheduling day-time activities that promote camaraderie. The benefits of a pleasant and productive work environment are more than worth it!

1. Pick and promote a theme for the year. Build company events, perks, and rewards around the theme.

2. Set a room aside as a "Cyber Café." Employees can socialize and use laptops during lunch, breaks, and before and after work. Provide free coffee and soft drinks. Add chalk or whiteboards, flip charts and markers for impromptu brainstorming sessions.

3. Throw a Valentine's Day "mocktail party" on February 14th. Non-alcoholic drinks are served along with Valentine cookies and other snacks.

4. Tell employees that they can paint and decorate their work areas. One New Jersey manager arrived one morning to find his team area decorated like the Hawaiian Islands. Another manager's team adopted a Club Med® look.

5. Turn a popular game into a motivational tool with team competition. Consider *Who Wants to Be a Millionaire®*, *Survivor®*, or *Jeopardy®*. Recognize winning teams in company newsletters, broadcast e-mails, and bulletin boards.

6. Hold an "appreciation event" for another department in recognition of support that was given on a joint project. The "event" could be anything from an invitation to lunch to taking everyone bowling.

7. If you have a company softball team, open it up to spouses and significant others.

Camaraderie continued…

8. Teams of employees start jigsaw puzzles in December and compete to finish them before January 1.

9. Encourage your employees to bring their hobbies, interests, and passions to work. For example, an employee that enjoys juggling was seen practicing during breaks much to the delight of his co-workers.

10. During orientation, give newly hired employees a card with the names of everyone who works in the company. The new employee is to get the signatures of everyone on the list. It's a great ice-breaker and super way for everyone to get to know the new "kids" on the block. Or do what one company does. All new hires get a "passport" and have a certain number of days to get their passport stamped by people in every department.

11. One company purchased and placed a grand piano in the lobby of the corporate office for all employees to enjoy. It's become a gathering place for employees during lunch and after work with talented employees taking turns entertaining their co-workers.

12. At a manufacturing plant, honeybees were discovered on company property. Rather than destroy them, several interested employees took responsibility for the hives. Every time honey is harvested, the company holds a pancake breakfast for all employees.

13. Consider employee Olympic Games. Some hotels do this and employees compete in the following: bed making, towel folding, key sorting, housekeeping cart relay, commode seat change, egg cracking, table busing, wine relay, and drink mixing. Get creative and offer something that is meaningful to *your* employees.

14. Re-create your founding year. This is a great reason to celebrate. Employees dress like people did at the time of the company founding. Decorate and play music of the times. Display scrapbooks, photos, and other memorabilia.

15. Throw a surprise party to celebrate the New Year complete with decorations, hats, noisemakers, confetti, and plenty of traditional party food. Everyone stops working at 3 p.m., or if you have multiple shifts, one to two hours before the shift ends. If you serve alcohol, be sure to provide transportation for those who may need assistance.

16. Keep in touch with your employees and encourage them to keep in touch with people they interface with that work in other departments. One company calls this type of contact "Howdy Visits." It's one way they work to stay in contact with one another. The manager uses his "Howdy Visits" to find out what his employees have on their minds.

20

Camaraderie continued…

17. Make this a ritual for one week: employees write down one silly thing they said, did, saw, or heard every day of the week. At the end of the week, everyone shares what he or she wrote.

18. Place a "camaraderie box" filled with post-it-notes®, stickers, colorful markers, etc. Encourage employees to acknowledge each other for any reason or no reason at all.

19. Treat your employees to a rafting trip. Trips can range from one day to longer than a week. Some outfitters set up camp and cook all of the meals, while others expect guests to participate. Many outfitters and river guides take inexperienced rafters down some of America's most beautiful rivers. Each company has its own style regarding pace, meals, and campsites. Try calling: American River Tourist Association at: 1-800-323-2782, www.arta.org or Dvorak's Kayak and Rafting Expeditions at: 1-800-824-3795, www.dvorakexpeditions.com or Outdoor Adventure River Specialists (OARS) at: 1-800-346-6277, www.oars.com.

20. Pass out napkins and kickoff a crazy brainstorming session. Employees record their ideas on paper napkins. Ideas are collected and discussed over soft drinks and snacks or lunch.

21. A team of employees, tired of their drab cubicles, decided to work "out in the open." They decorated the ceiling with over 600 multi-colored lights. They had M&M® lights, character lights, pig lights, skeleton lights, Crayon® lights, and flashing lights. As a result, they no longer use the fluorescent lights that they hated.

22. Treat your employees to a weekend at a Dude Ranch. Horseback riding is just one of the many activities they offer. There are rodeos, fishing, tennis, hiking, and spa treatments. At sundown there are chuck wagon dinners, square dances, yodeling contests, and bonfires. To find a good fit for your employees and your budget, contact: The Dude Ranchers' Association, 307-587-2339, www.duderanch.org.

23. Head for an overnight camping trip with your employees and their families. Family camps offer programs for adults and children of all ages and are becoming increasingly popular. One standout is Tyler Place Family Resort in Highgate Springs, Vermont. They can be reached at 802-868-4000, or via their web site: www.tylerplace.com. Guests stay in cottages or lodge suites and can choose from biking, hiking, kayaking, canoeing, water skiing, and tennis. The kids join their age groups that meet from 8:30 a.m. to 1:30 p.m. and from 5:30 p.m. to 8:30 p.m. Activities include everything from swimming and pony rides to pajama parties and camp-outs.

24. Allow the team to sign their work before the product or paperwork leaves the company. This could be with initials of each team member on a card or note tag.

Camaraderie continued…

25. To promote teamwork and encourage servers to accurately report tips, one restaurant matches 5% of the total tips reported by employees. That amount is allocated among all hourly employees, based on hours worked, and is credited to each employee's account.

26. Write unpopular tasks on slips of paper and place the slips inside of balloons. Blow up the balloons. Have employees pop a balloon to find out who gets to do what for the day or week. Tasks might include cleaning out the coffeepot, supplying paper products to the restrooms, unjamming the copy machine, or changing the toner cartridge.

27. Hold employee meetings for non-management employees. Oftentimes staff meetings include only management personnel. Try including your non-management employees at least once a month if you have weekly meetings. Distribute an agenda in advance.

28. During a particularly low sales period, the manager of a demoralized telemarketing team asked everybody to work under their desks for an hour. The energy changed and the team met its goals for the day.

29. Fill a jar with marbles or pennies. Each team member who reaches a goal for the week can guess how many marbles or pennies are in the jar. When all of the guesses are turned in the exact number is revealed. The five people who guess the exact number or come closest win a prize.

30. Set a daily goal that is achievable, but one the team will have to "stretch" to meet. Then draw a circle on a whiteboard that represents a pizza. Divide it into 8 pieces. For every 1/8 of the daily goal the team reaches, color in a segment. When the entire "pizza" is colored in, order pizza for the entire team!

31. Each team of employees draws a color from a hat. The next day, everyone wears and decorates using their "team colors" for the day. Give each team a small budget for decorations.

32. Hold "Communication Briefings" with your team of employees. Buy a popcorn machine and serve popcorn and soft drinks while the manager or director shares the latest information. Allow time for a question and answer session.

33. Each team works to earn letters to spell a word that is related to their work. For example, "budget" might be a word. The team can earn the "b" if they meet their sales goal for the day. They can earn the "u" if they surpass the sales goal for the day, etc. This contest could last anywhere from one day to several weeks or even months.

22

Camaraderie continued…

34. Hold a "Slogan Week." Teams are given materials to create a slogan banner. The slogan must represent a philosophy as related to customer service, increased sales, accurate accounting, etc. They have one week to complete the assignment.

35. For each goal the team meets they get to take a Lego® piece. You may want to award more than one piece for especially tough goals. The first team to "build" a car or house or whatever the teams decide on wins.

36. Get your employees involved in mentoring or being a buddy to new employees. They will not only help the company and new employees, but also themselves. It will give them an opportunity to reach out to others, share information, and shorten the learning curve for new hires. Keep in mind that a buddy program looks deceptively simple, but it is not. It isn't rocket science, yet it goes beyond common sense. You're better off not to start a program unless you have the time and resources to do it right. However, done right, when getting your entire team involved, will give you a win-win for everyone.

37. Support an *Employee Retention Council.* Everyone benefits when turnover is kept to a minimum. This cross-section of employees meets as a team to discuss ways to reduce employee turnover.

38. Invite your employees to an Outdoor Wilderness Leadership School. Companies that have done this have found that rugged outdoor challenges can topple rigid office hierarchies and encourage the sort of camaraderie often missing from traditional off-site work events.

39. Teams of employees were invited to make their own bowling shirts. The company bought the shirts and the teams designed the shirts. They all wore their shirts to the local bowling alley for 6 hours of fun including prizes for the best and worst shirt designs.

40. Hold a team meeting in an unusual place. One manager held his meeting at a gas station. Another time he gathered everyone together in the produce department of a local grocery store. He's also asked his team to submit suggestions for off-the-wall meeting places.

41. Introduce support staff to customers by taking them on sales calls. Support staff seldom get to meet the customers they speak with by phone. It's a great morale booster.

42. Surprise your employees and turn the lunch break with your team into fix-your-own peanut butter and jelly sandwiches.

Chapter 4 - Incentives for Growth

*"It's not enough to tell people they should be happy to have a job here.
At a time when people are asked to stretch themselves with fewer
resources, you want to reward them for that stretch."*

—Bruce Donatuti, Director of HR

People naturally want to grow—in their work and in their lives. Give them the opportunity to do both. When employees seek out growth in their jobs or areas of expertise, or in anything that personally interests them, the end result is a happier and more productive employee who becomes even more valuable to the company. Employees are more apt to stay for the long term with an organization that provides opportunities to learn new things.

Inspire your employees with incentives to grow. Below you'll find many ways to offer encouragement that are simple, innovative, and expansive. Assume success and watch it become a self-filling prophecy. Do whatever you can to encourage your employees to reach their full potential. It's a benefit for both the employee and the manager.

Promote growth by listening more and talking less, soliciting suggestions and giving less advice, praising more and criticizing less, and asking questions as you seek to understand their point of view. Never penalize honest mistakes.

1. Let employees set their own salaries. Companies that have done this found that people know what they're worth in the marketplace and don't tend to overrate themselves. Management reserves the right to accept or reject the proposed salary.

2. Offer karate classes so that your employees can learn self-defense, improve coordination, flexibility, and self-awareness, while staying physically fit.

3. Setup a technical track to let scientists or other technical employees advance without taking on management tasks. That way they don't have to become managers to move up.

4. Invite local college and university representatives to meet with your employees on-site and discuss with them courses of study that might be of interest. This is a great way to further education by bringing the information to them.

5. Regularly post information on the company's financial status on a bulletin board. Data might include revenue growth, expenses, sales figures, comparison with competitors or industry, and other trends and key performance measures. Avoid using technical jargon because it might be confusing to some people.

24

Incentives for Growth continued…

6. March is the month for the annual American Red Cross CPR Saturday. Sponsor training in adult CPR. It takes only four hours and your employees will learn how to save a life. Call: 1-800-733-2767.

7. Declare a "Let's Learn Something New Day." Employees plan activities for this special day of professional growth.

8. Offer fitness opportunities that include aerobics, weight training, golf lessons, Tai Chi, and Yoga.

9. Give each employee a monthly book allowance. This is money that your employees *must* spend *only* on reading materials for themselves.

10. Provide tuition reimbursement for *anything* the employee wishes to study. One employee studied taxidermy which she planned to pursue upon retirement.

11. Establish a program to move technical knowledge from junior to senior managers. Many of today's executives are not familiar with all of the newest in technological advances. Name a junior board of directors to advise on and execute technology-related decisions. The board may be advisory, but it can still carry weight in terms of suggestions. A company that has a program in place calls this sharing of information "e-mentoring." Their executives say they are now more comfortable with the terrain that comes with the new economy.

12. Hold an "internal job fair" for your current employees. Interview applicants to fill vacant positions just as you do when hiring from outside your organization. This could be a half-day event or last several days, depending upon the number of vacancies and number of interested employees.

13. Provide employees an opportunity to meet with "life coaches" to help employees learn how to balance home, life, and work.

14. In one company, every new employee is assigned a mentor based upon common interests. During each of the quarterly performance reviews during the first year, both the immediate supervisor *and* the mentor complete and deliver the performance evaluation. Employees like having their mentor involved in providing feedback. In some cases, the mentor knows the employee better than the supervisor does.

15. Organize a Trivia Quiz Party. The Master of Ceremony develops sets of twenty questions. Questions are related to product knowledge, policies and procedures for various tasks, etc. Teams are given one set of questions at a time and have fifteen minutes to answer each set. The teams with the most correct answers win.

16. Offer a Weight Watchers® at work program.

25

Incentives for Growth continued...

17. A corporate training company was hired to teach boating basics to a team of 20 employees who then competed in a sailboat race in the New York Harbor.

18. Do away with all job titles to take away the perception that a title makes the person.

19. Divide into two teams. Present an action, behavior, or a skill that that needs improvement or learning. Start with the first team. Ask for one benefit that will be gained from the action, behavior, or skill. Write the answer on flipchart paper. Move to the next team. Record their answer. Allow 15 to 30 minutes. All ideas are acceptable, even the off-the-wall ideas. Discuss the benefits they suggest.

20. One company held a brown-paper fair. They used a big, multi-purpose room at their headquarters and taped up brown butcher paper all over the walls. On the paper was a flow chart of their work process. They invited everyone in the company to put up anonymous post-it-notes® telling them which parts of the process were working, which were not, and why.

21. Employees earn a playing card for showing up on time each day. At the end of the week employees play their best poker hand and the winner gets a prize.

22. Create daily affirmations. Maybe it's in the form of 3x5 cards with a note from one employee to another or a special quotation that can be passed among co-workers.

23. Establish a "floating" assignment system that allows employees to bid for projects in other departments.

24. Send your employees to a movie in the middle of the afternoon. However, the movie must be one that offers a message. The next day the team meets to share ideas from the movie that will help their team reach their goals. Teams present their ideas to the other teams in a group meeting.

25. Form a "Culture Shift" team to lead the company or department in a new direction. Build in lots of activities and fun. Most people have a tough time adjusting to change. Get your employees "buy-in" and involvement in making it happen.

26. Hold a "boot camp" for new-hires that includes a comprehensive new-hire orientation.

27. Support a "Time Wasters" committee. Members identify time-wasting activities, reports, and processes. Ideas are presented to management for consideration and possible elimination.

28. Get your bank to hold a free financial seminar on topics of interest to your employees.

Incentives for Growth continued...

29. Give your employees a chance to make partner while working part-time, as did Deloitte & Touche in the 1990s.

30. Setup a learning lab were employees can go to improve their reading and writing skills.

31. Create a formal mentoring program to match employees with executives they wouldn't ordinarily have access to. Mentees are chosen on the basis of their leadership potential.

32. Offer technical fellowships to engineers who get research budgets and then provide them with broad latitude to work on special projects.

33. Build a "cave" where your employees have privacy to write, think, talk on the phone, and meet as a team to work on tough problems.

34. Provide off-site special locations just for "techies."

35. Give employees the chance to shine publicly by putting them in charge of highly visible projects.

36. Pick one or two people to "grow." Make them your special project and help them in every way you can. (You don't need to tell them you're doing this).

37. Send promising managers to management development programs that are offered at business schools.

38. Show your employees that you value their judgment and opinions by including employees in your decision making process.

39. Start a book club that meets on employee time (during lunch, or before or after work).

40. Provide attractive relocation packages for current employees as well as new-hires.

41. Get rid of your dictatorial managers and replace them with managers who know how to coach, encourage, and empower. It's one of the best ways to let your employees know that you value and respect them. Poor managers are the morale busters that often destroy organizations and the people who work for them.

42. Offer your employees a chance to transfer oversees if you're a global company.

43. Be flexible with regard to sick leave and vacation, especially during times of major change. Just make sure you don't show favoritism.

27

Incentives for Growth continued…

44.	Compensate fairly. Employees do not necessarily need to feel rich, but they want to feel they are paid along the lines of other people doing the same or similar work if you're going to get their best from them.

45.	People work best when working toward tangible goals or when building something that leads to an outcome they can see. Make sure your employees have a clear vision of where the organization is headed. Communicate that vision from the top on down.

46.	A restaurant adds 50 cents to employees' hourly pay for each new skill they learn. Employees have the chance to cross-train in different areas from janitorial to kitchen prep. The program is optional, but most employees are eager to join in.

47.	Make sure that at the core of your personnel policy there is a procedure whereby employee complaints can be heard and, if necessary, appealed right up to the Chairman.

48.	Trust your employees to do what's right. Get rid of traditional policies and procedures. Recognize employees for their efforts even if they are not always successful.

49.	Invite the janitor to a staff meeting or anyone else who can provide a new perspective on a problem.

50.	Let employees bid on jobs that would ordinarily be done by an outside contractor such as lawn and garden care of the company grounds or janitorial services. You might be surprised at how many employees are capable of doing this work and are interested in earning extra money.

51.	Anticipate that people learn at different rates of speed. As much as we would like everyone to grasp new ideas quickly, that's not always reality. Don't expect every new concept to be learned with the first explanation.

52.	Encourage and help your employees to respond to setbacks with renewed effort. It's the long-term key to growth and success.

53.	An employer bought boxing gloves and invited an instructor to teach cardio-boxing after work to interested employees.

54.	Ask your employees for their opinions. Everyone likes to give advice. This can be done informally or with a formal department or company-wide program.

55.	Make work-related travel optional for employees who typically travel. If employees can find a way to get the job done without traveling, let them do it.

56.   Invite a favorite local high school or college coach to give a pep talk to your employees, as did a company in North Carolina. A number of years ago they surprised their employees with a visit from the late Jimmy Valvano, the coach of the North Carolina State University championship basketball team.

57.   One hospital gave each of their employees a calendar of health observation and recognition dates for the health, medical, and hospital industry. Dates are included for public awareness of healthcare issues as well as recognition dates for healthcare professionals. For example, January is National Eye Care Month among other things. February is American Heart Month among other things. Contact: Pam Pohly Associates at: www.pohly.com or e-mail her at: resumes@pohly.com.

58.   Ask questions. Find out what part of your employee's jobs take up the most time. What report(s) do they create that no one uses? What is the most frustrating aspect of their job? Ask for the problems and then do something about it. Give them the credit for identifying the issues.

59.   Let your employees know it's okay to make mistakes. Tell them that. We all make mistakes; it's a part of being human. Don't count mistakes as crimes.

60.   Suggestion programs can be invaluable. However, if you have or plan to implement a suggestion program, be sure you plan ahead. If you don't, you run the risk of alienating your employees rather than motivating them to get involved.

61.   Remember that no single accomplishment lasts forever. Without continued learning, today's success is only a memory. Encourage your employees to seek out new challenges and seize opportunities for growth. You can do this best by setting a good example.

62.   Contract with your local community college to send instructors to your company and teach classes after hours. It's a cost-effective way to offer training in a convenient, in-house setting.

63.   Outstanding restaurant employees are invited to attend an annual educational trip to the Napa Valley that includes winery visits and fine dining.

64.   Start a mandatory reading club. Once a week or month, have a "reading meeting." Require each employee to bring one article that they think could have an impact on how the company does business. Have them summarize the article, and then discuss it as a group.

29

Chapter 5 - Freebies

"Workers deserve not only wages,
but roses as well."

—Walter Kohler Sr.
President of Kohler Co. until 1941

Freebies are the things you give your employees just because they're your employees. They aren't rewards, awards, or recognition that have to be earned. They're "perks" and benefits you offer as added value.

Freebies are a token of your appreciation—for no special reason. These "perks" and benefits are for employees at all levels of the company to enjoy. Freebies may not cost the company much, but they can seem like "champagne, a box of fancy chocolates, and roses" every day of the year to the people who work for you.

1. Provide coffee stations on every floor of the building. Serve free coffee and tea.

2. Provide a certain number of "family sick days" which allow employees to stay home and care for sick children and/or relatives.

3. A company in the Midwest installed a small music system so that warehouse employees have music on the loading dock.

4. Offer paid holidays to part-time as well as full time employees.

5. Arrange for low-cost financial benefits for your employees through your company's bank. Perks might include free checking, lower interest rates, special discounts on approved loans, or credit card finance charges.

6. Offer health benefits to domestic partners of eligible employees. This includes same-sex and live-in opposite-sex couples.

7. Provide stock options that include accelerated vesting—in one year instead of three years.

8. Purchase an annual membership for each of your employees to Sam's Club or Costco. This is an inexpensive perk that employees are reminded of every time they shop at one of these discount warehouses.

9. Install a sauna as did California-based SSH Communications Security, Inc. Their employees enjoy taking a break inside the office in their eight-person sauna. Provide a towel service.

Freebies continued...

10. Let your employees take up to 40 hours of unpaid leave per year to use as they please.

11. Raise the retail discount for employees from 40 percent to 50 percent.

12. Offer a database of reputable service providers for your employees to access that might include: electricians, plumbers, doctors, dentists, antique dealers, jewelers, house cleaners, roofers, house painters, window washers, chimney sweeps, landscapers, tree trimmers, and other seasonal services unique to your area. This is particularly important if you have new employees joining you from outside of the country, the state, or your community.

13. Pass out favorite childhood candy. Include popular candy from a variety of generations.

14. Provide escort/security services for employees that work late or after dark.

15. Provide umbrellas for employees to use when it rains unexpectedly.

16. Designate several "privacy phones" where employees can make personal, local calls during lunch and breaks.

17. Give *everyone* stock options. Employees that have a stake in the company are more likely to stick with you.

18. Put a decorated shoebox on your desk and fill it with candy. It gives employees an excuse to drop by. It's another way to stay in touch with your staff.

19. Let your employees use lawyers just as they do doctors in a company health plan via a prepaid legal plan. Through a payroll deduction, employees pay a relatively low monthly fee. They then have access to thousands of lawyers in the network.

20. For parents that prefer at-home child care, put them in touch with nanny services and provide funding for that care just as you do with an on-site child care center.

21. Implement a 24-hour voice mail hotline to let employees ask questions, complain, share concerns, and ideas.

22. Charter buses to pick up employees from rapid transit park-and-ride lots so they don't have to make the daily trek up traffic-choked roads.

23. Offer your employees a consultation with an ergonomic engineer who will customize the employee's work environment, reduce the risks of injury, and improve productivity.

Freebies continued…

24. Include laser eye surgery as a part of your regular healthcare package.

25. Allow your employees to order their groceries on-line for delivery to their vehicles at the end of the day in the company parking lot.

26. Provide a handyman service. While employees are working, small repairs are made in their homes up to a specified dollar amount.

27. Build an outside structure such as a large gazebo where employees can work on warm days. Install LAN and telephone jacks in the structure so employees can stay connected.

28. Provide your employees with a complete 800+ megahertz PC and printer system delivered to any employee's home. The system comes with built-in access to both the Internet and the company's Intranet through web access.

29. Pay for cellular phones for your employees that they may use for both business and personal reasons.

30. Provide cafeteria compensation plans that offer options for work arrangements, as well as alternatives for pensions and retiree healthcare benefits.

31. Set up a "carb" table in the break room with pretzels, popcorn, energy bars, soy nuts, and other foods to keep your employees energized.

32. Provide on-site ATM machines.

33. Offer eldercare as an optional, subsidized benefit.

34. Provide free uniforms for employees that are required to wear them.

35. Provide free lunch for all employees *every* day.

36. Help pay for the cost of adoption of a child. The most common adoption benefits are referral services and cost reimbursement. One company offers its employees up to $5,000 in costs and provides all parents-to-be with counseling and flexible schedules. Another pays up to $20,000 in costs, gives six weeks' paid leave, a bonus vacation week, a scholarship fund of $2,500, and a "new arrival" sign for the new parent's office door.

37. Offer pet health insurance as a before tax employee benefit.

38. Make a commitment to physical fitness by providing tennis, basketball, and volleyball courts.

Freebies continued…

39.   Give your team a budget of $50 each month to use as they feel appropriate. Several teams may wish to pool their money for office supplies or equipment beyond what is furnished.

40.   Allow employees to use UPS and Federal Express services for personal use. Employees pay for services but at the corporate discount rate.

41.   Offer free shoe repair services on-site or hire a service that picks up and delivers.

42.   Provide the following: florist, travel agent, tailoring, photo processing, discount tickets, and drivers license renewal on-site or nearby.

43.   Treat your employees to an annual transportation allowance.

44.   Provide free on-site mammograms for women and free PSA tests for men.

45.   Provide a room with soft music and chaise lounges so employees can recline and relax. Those who wish to talk on a cell phone or work using a laptop can do so as well.

46.   Arrange for a pay-for-view sporting event that your employees can enjoy either at work or in their own home.

47.   Surprise your employees with fruit smoothies.

48.   Lease cars for your employees to drive for three years with an option to buy thereafter.

49.   Pay for preparation of employees' wills.

50.   Surprise your employees with M&M®s in the breakroom.

51.   Offer a 10-hour day, 4 days-a-week option or even a 12-hour day, 3 days-a-week.

52.   Join an employee cruise club such as that offered by Royal Caribbean International. You'll receive posters and brochures designed for your employees with special discount coupons. When your employees and their guests take advantage of cruise club discounts, the company will earn credit toward complimentary cruises. Use bonus cruises for employee drawings. Contact: Royal Caribbean at: 1-888-520-7225.

53.   Surprise your employees with a coupon. On it write, "Good For" and include things such as lunch with the supervisor, one-half day off with pay, a free tank of gas, or whatever your employees might enjoy.

Freebies continued...

54. Provide concierge services to include waiting for service people at home, shuttling children to after-school events, and running assorted errands.

55. Allow employees to place orders and take-home meals from the company cafeteria.

56. Handout "Paycheck" candy bars on payday along with payroll checks.

57. Offer a "Mom Shift" that runs from 9 a.m. to 2 p.m. in order to accommodate mothers or fathers of school-age children.

58. If you have to downsize, be sure you have a safety net in place. Outplacement services can be an invaluable resource to someone that finds out that they no longer have a job. It also sends the message to all employees that you take care of your employees to the end.

59. Designate a room for naps. When employees are tired, they can take a nap or simply relax.

60. Fill the office with holiday scents: potpourri, fresh-cut pine boughs, and scented candles.

61. Fly the employee's spouse or significant other to the job site if the employee must work out-of-town for a long period of time.

62. Surprise your employees with funny screen savers for their computers.

63. Surprise your employees with a special mouse pad designed by the creative members of your team or get everyone involved in the artwork.

64. Hire an ice cream truck and servers to park on company property and serve your employees in honor of a special event or as a surprise.

65. Serve "finger" sandwiches made with fancy cookie cutters.

66. Have all of your employees' cars washed while they are working.

67. Provide pet treats for your employees' pets.

68. For companies that hire foreign nationals, make sure that you help them get off to a good start both professionally and personally. This may even mean assisting them in setting up housekeeping.

69. One company built a sports bar in the middle of its high-rise offices, complete with a big-screen television and free beer on tap (allowed after hours only).

Freebies continued...

70. One company photographed their employees all year long and surprised each of them at the end of the year with a photo calendar that had a picture of every employee on his or her own page. Extra pages were used for meaningful quotations.

71. When starting Daylight Savings time in the Spring, let employees go home an hour early on Friday or come in an hour late on Monday (with pay) to "make up" for the "shortened" weekend.

72. Hire someone to roam about the company giving free shoeshines.

73. Offer wallpaper options for all computers including the American flag and patriotic symbols.

74. Don't charge retirees that choose to participate in company events dues or fees, or charge a discounted amount.

75. Pay for 100 percent of healthcare premiums for your employees and 50 percent of the cost for family members. Employees who do not need the benefits because they are covered by a spouse's plan, may "bank" the money to be used toward sick-day pay.

76. A hotel management company makes rooms available at a modest cost ($25 per room, per night) to employees and their immediate family members. They manage hotels throughout the U.S. and employees at all levels in the company value this perk.

77. A company with a child care center for employees' children had child-size tables and chairs set up in the company cafeteria so that the children may join their parents for lunch or eat with the other children as a group at their own table.

78. Send a cookie gram to your team of employees for meeting their goals for the month.

79. Buy a "Pin the Tail on the Donkey" game. Every time an employee meets a goal they get a tail to pin on the donkey. At the end of the day or week, take turns blindfolding employees and play, "Pin the Tail on the Donkey". The person who pins closest to the tail wins a prize. The more tails they have the more chances to win.

Chapter 6 - Fun Stuff

"Give into the power of goofiness. It lets the mind relax and catch its breath. Only goofiness has the inherent power to keep seriousness from killing off all of your ideas. Ripples of laughter will wash up the brightest gems on the shore of your consciousness. I believe there is a least one angel named 'Goofy.' In the hierarchy, it is definitely a higher-level angel."

—Dalton Roberts, Columnist
Chattanooga, TN - Times Free Press

Let the good times roll! Occasional fun and humor can re-energize your employees from the daily grind of work. It doesn't take much. Things such as a "Friday fluorescent sock day" or a "roving kazoo band" of managers entertaining employees at lunch can provide many laughs and uplift your employees—at no cost to the company. although it may "cost" a few managers some red faces!

Or you can take it to the next level. Bring in a mime or balloon artist to amuse your staff throughout the day. Rent or buy a jukebox filled with "oldies" for the lunchroom. Turn the lunchroom floor into a dance floor so your employees can "boogie" at lunch to the music of the 50s and 60s. Yes, these things cost money. Yet the benefits of having happy, loyal, and productive people who look forward to coming to work is more than worth it. Like children, adults learn through play; for children, play is thought of as a rehearsal for life; for adults, it's part of what makes life and work interesting and worthwhile.

You can also do "fun stuff" after hours. Rent a limousine(s) to chauffeur your employees to a local comedy club show. Hold a masquerade ball at the local lodge where employees come dressed up as their alter egos. Create a company reputation of being a fun place to work. Here are some ideas to help you make that happen.

1. Sponsor a rodeo on company time or after hours complete with country music, cowboy (girl) hats, rodeo games, a chuck wagon with food, and a mechanical bull.

2. Hold a post-holiday party. To cut down on the frenzy and prolong the joy of the season, schedule a special event for your employees *after* the December holidays.

3. May 5th is Cinco de Mayo. Decorate. Celebrate. Let your employees take turns swinging at a giant pinata filled with candy, T-shirts, and gift certificates. Pinatas, which date back to 16th century Italy, are made of papier-mache and come in every conceivable size and shape. You can even take a whack at Superman or Darth Vader. For those who want to have fun with the boss, you can order a custom-make look-alike pinata.

Fun Stuff continued...

4. At one company, employees that have been recognized by customers and/or colleagues during the month are given a chance to spin a large roulette wheel and win a prize. The prizes are not expensive; employees have a budget and decide what prizes appear on the wheel. This activity is fun but it also reinforces the importance of good customer service.

5. A Southern California company held a "day in winter" event. Employees wore winter clothing to work. They decorated with snow shovels, artificial snow, ice skates, sleds, skis, and potbelly stoves. They served chili and hot chocolate. It was an 80-degree January day and everyone had a great time.

6. Throw a "Thank Goodness It's Friday" party. The price of admission is "one idea, frivolous or serious, to make the company a more fun place to work." Suggestions are submitted in advance and shared at the party.

7. Sponsor a "bring your pet to work day." Be sure you have plenty of pet treats on hand along with litter boxes, scoops, and disposable bags.

8. Provide art and craft supplies, (paints and brushes, markers, chalk, clay, scissors, construction paper, pencils, string, tape, sequins, beads, thread, buttons, rick-rack, ribbon, colorful pipe cleaners, and glue). Employees who choose to get creative during breaks, lunch, and before and after work can do so.

9. Sponsor a "Chili Dump" or call it "Chili for One." Every employee who wants to participate makes one gallon of chili to dump into a huge pot for sharing. The flavors blend and the chili is delicious. Employees who participated got five one dollar raffle tickets for a drawing at the end of the day.

10. Declare a "Fun Day" and plan special fun events throughout the day. This could include: free donuts and coffee in the morning, a pizza party at noon, and cookies and fruit in the afternoon.

11. Take your employees "junking." Spend the day or half-day shopping flea markets, Goodwill and Salvation Army stores, garage sales, or anywhere they are likely to find interesting bargains.

12. Hold a fishing contest to see who can catch the biggest fish of whatever abundant species are in your local lakes. This takes place during the entire fishing season. Employees bring their catch to work to be weighed on a certified scale. At the end of the fishing season, prizes are awarded to the winners.

13. Tension was building. Everyone was on the verge of losing it. A punching clown arrived in the breakroom. It relieved the stress and everyone had fun letting off steam.

37

Fun Stuff continued...

14. For a break in the middle of the day, have employees divide into two teams. Give each team 100 Ping-Pong balls. They have three minutes to toss the balls at the other team. The team with the fewest number of Ping-Pong balls on their side when time is up wins.

15. Hold a "Fortune Teller Party" complete with palm and card readings, Ouija boards, and a crystal ball. Party favors could include horoscope books, mystical ornaments, zodiac signs, and other fun items.

16. A company in Australia installed a 3-story slide for the entertainment of their employees at the company's new headquarters. It even has a kink about halfway down, increasing the sensation of speed.

17. Hold a "Hats Off to Spring" party. Employees wear a variety of hats including top hats, straw hats, bonnets, and caps. Prizes are awarded for the most sophisticated hat, unusual decoration, authentic style, funniest, and most creative use of natural materials.

18. Employees of one company met the challenge in a cardboard boat Regatta. Teams of employees built boats made from corrugated cardboard, paper, tape, glue, paint and lots of imagination. The human powered boats had to be capable of completing at least three laps around a 200-yard course. Prizes were awarded to the winners in several categories.

19. Hold a "standup" meeting every morning to give everyone a chance to share with the rest of their team what he or she is working on. A "standup" meeting is quick, to the point, and an energizer. No one sits down.

20. Create an internal on-line database of jokes, cartoons, and other funny material. Employees that have something to share can contribute to the database. This idea helps reduce unnecessary e-mails and spamming.

21. Hold a Spring plant trade event whereby employees who enjoy gardening can trade seedlings, bulbs, and plants with one another.

22. Fill a room with containers of bubbles, clown noses, wax lips and teeth, Groucho glasses, and stress balls. Watch them have fun!

23. Liven up your memos. Buy a book of one-liners, and include a joke at the bottom of your memos.

24. Send your employees out for a "fun lunch." Tell them not to worry about how long they're gone. The only rule is that they are not allowed to talk about work or they must pay for their own lunch.

38

Fun Stuff continued…

25. Allow your employees to decorate the hallways with "Trash Art." Included is *anything* that's not offensive. There will be original artwork as well as posters and cartoons clipped from newspapers and magazines. You probably will also see pictures of employees' pets, friends, children, and co-workers.

26. Give an employee(s) an opportunity to run away and join the circus. Camp Winnarainbow, 150 miles north of San Francisco is just the place. It's a performing arts camp for "kids" of all ages. The adult program is nine days in June before the kids takeover. The main attractions are the opportunity to learn to ride a unicycle, walk on stilts or a tight rope, juggle, or fly on a cloud swing. For those who want to clown around, the costume and makeup areas are also very popular. Contact their web site at: www.campwinnarainbow.org or call: 510-525-4304.

27. Rent a houseboat for a departmental party. Provide fishing equipment and bait as well as sunscreen, food, and beverages.

28. Hold a Scrabble® tournament for an afternoon. The winner wins a necklace or trophy made with scrabble tiles.

29. On the computers' screen saver, compile a product knowledge quiz that changes every day. When employees are not using their computers, a question will automatically appear on their screen. At the end of the week answers to the questions appear and employees with the most correct answers win a prize.

30. Hold a "Christmas in July" party complete with holiday food and music, a tree, gift exchange, and anything else to make the party festive. One company even produced its own snow and everyone joined together to build a snowman.

31. A manager who wanted to "step outside of the box" invited her employees to step outside of an airplane at 14,000 feet. Those who participated called it their "sky-high" bonding experience and can't wait to jump again.

32. One department manager gave each of his employees rose-colored glasses to help them look at failures and mistakes as learning experiences.

33. A manager holds a staff meeting in a bathrobe and slippers to kickoff creative thinking with his or her team.

34. The owner of one company surprised her employees by having them picked up one afternoon in an open-air tram that took them on a picnic to a private park where food, drinks, and entertainment were provided.

35. Hold a "Bring Your Teddy Bear to Work Day."

39

Fun Stuff continued...

36. Hold a sandcastle building contest in your company parking lot. Have sand delivered and watch your employees get creative. Award prizes in a variety of categories.

37. At an upscale natural foods grocery chain, staff members wear huge, handmade nametags with cartoons and fun letters that reflect the personality of the wearer.

38. In a manufacturing plant, a trumpet call is broadcast on the public address system and everyone does a set of light exercises. It's a little crazy, but it's a great stress reliever.

39. Invite a storyteller to entertain your employees as part of a company-wide meeting.

40. Hold a balsa-wood airplane construction and flying contest to celebrate achievement of a team goal.

41. On a teacher workday (when children have off from school), sponsor a field trip. Volunteers chaperon kids on a trip to a museum, the zoo, or other place of special interest to children.

42. Ask a "Stupid Question Day" occurs during the month of October. Get creative and use this opportunity to have fun.

43. One manager at a bank asked a local bakery to frost and decorate hamburger buns. For a surprise Friday morning celebration, she posted a banner that read: "Thanks for working your buns off this week!"

44. Regularly orchestrate offbeat workplace celebrations. One company celebrated Willie Nelson's birthday and all of the employees wore bandanas.

45. Transform your factory or office into a city-like environment, as did Nortel at their global telecommunications headquarters in Brampton, a suburb of Toronto. They have two main arteries—Main Street and Colonnade, seven indoor parks, a Zen garden, a dry-cleaner, a bank, basketball and volleyball courts, and a wide variety of cafes and restaurants.

46. Invite your employees to enter a home video contest. The video may not be longer than 5 minutes. Award prizes in a variety of categories such as funniest, craziest, most creative, animals, and children. Invite a local television producer to judge the contest or leave it up to your employees.

47. Employees were let off from work one hour early on March 4th (Get it? March forth!) Employees left to the tune of a kazoo band of managers playing "Stars and Stripes Forever."

Fun Stuff continued...

48. One manager offered two free seats to a professional basketball game in his town for the employee who wrote him the funniest memo that day.

49. Start a lending library of framed artwork. Employees change the artwork on their office walls once a quarter. Charge a nominal fee to make initial purchases of popular prints of classic, modern, and selected art posters. Encourage employees to donate art to the library. A committee determines appropriateness of each lending piece.

50. Start Monday mornings with a "two minute warning." Employees meet in the conference room for a scheduled staff meeting. As an incentive for prompt attendance, a $50 bill is awarded to the person whose phone extension is drawn at random—providing he or she can answer a question from the employee handbook.

51. Hold a contest to see who can tag the biggest buck. This takes place during both rifle and bow-hunting season. The size is determined by measuring the horns using agreed upon methodology.

52. Hold a balloon bodybuilder contest. To play, separate employees into teams of four or five players. The object of the game is to stuff as many balloons inside of their clothing as they can in 3 minutes without popping any. "Bodybuilders" model their physiques to the judges who determine the winners. Don't forget a camera!

53. Designate a relaxation room that employees can paint, decorate, and use during breaks. One team of employees decorated the room with glow-in-the dark paint, beanbag chairs, and long strands of beads covering the doorway. This wild and fun place gave employees an escape from their stressful jobs and provided a relaxing place to meet.

54. Consider a "Laugh Mobile" like the one that rolls through the oncology department at Duke University Medical Center in Durham, North Carolina several times each week. They dispense audio-tapes of stand-up comedians and props such as water guns to patients (nurses are popular targets).

55. One company has a "rumors" bulletin board in the employee meeting room. When employees hear rumors, they jot them down and post them. At regular staff meetings, managers read the rumors aloud and respond to them so that everyone gets "the scoop."

56. Come to work dressed as a Pilgrim and pass out "Happy Thanksgiving" buttons, as did one manager who surprised his employees.

57. The manager surprised his employees with caramel corn, popcorn and candy bars.

41

Fun Stuff continued…

58. Just for the fun of it, employees dressed up using a theme. At one high tech company, they all dressed up for the circus. In another company, they dressed in pairs or as a couple. In another company, they dressed as storybook characters.

59. Rent a frozen drink machine for a special event or just to surprise your employees on a hot summer day. Call Brian Meyer of *A Frozen Creation* in Atlanta, Georgia at: 770-587-3513 for more information.

60. Hold a "witches' brew" contest for Halloween. Employees are invited to submit their best soup or "brew" for judging and for everyone to enjoy.

61. Craft a birthday surprise. Team leader takes photos with a digital camera of each employee. Employees decorate a paper plate with their photo in the middle and surprise their manager on his or her birthday. Hilarious!

62. Fill clean trash cans with costumes and props. Employees have two hours to write, rehearse, and present a play, vignette, or commercial.

63. On the day new employees start work, give them a $75 gift certificate for a pair of running shoes as a reminder to always put themselves in the customer's shoes.

64. Offer a hip-hop dance or Latin cardio class after work.

65. Employees try to break a water balloon using their bodies, but no hands or feet.

66. When a new employee joins your organization welcome him or her with a special T-shirt signed by the other employees.

67. Name that tune. When a song is played on the public address system, employees can call in and name the tune. First correct answer wins a prize.

68. Sponsor a contest to write jingles about the goals of the department or company. Hold a "people's choice" vote after participants sing or perform the jingles. Everyone gets a vote for the top three.

69. Hold a "Nocturnal Easter Egg Hunt" for your employees' children as one company did in the South. Youngsters used flashlights to search for Easter candy and toy-filled eggs on the event lawn as well as eggs filled with some great prizes. The egg hunt began at 8 p.m. as advertised—rain or shine.

70. Give your employees a chance to win a limousine service for four hours on a Saturday evening.

Fun Stuff continued…

71. As an act of pure pampering, one manager asked his employees to join him in a 30-minute barefoot walk in the park across the street from their office. It was a great stress-reliever and totally unexpected which made it especially memorable.

72. Hit the slopes with your employees. For those that don't ski there are other activities including skating, sledding, swimming, tennis, and warming in front of the fireplace. Try Breckenridge, Colorado at: 1-800-789-7669, or contact their web site at: www.breckenridge.snow.com. Or try Squaw Valley, Lake Tahoe, California at: 1-800-401-9216, www.squaw.com or Waterville Valley, New Hampshire at: 1-800-468-2553, www.waterville.com.

73. Everyone is familiar with the causal dress work environment. Hold a "dress up" day.

74. An idea for family-oriented companies is "inn to inn" biking. Kid-oriented companies offer trips that your employees' children can take. A tour company provides bikes and helmets, schedules meals, and arranges for a van to carry luggage to inns each night. Call Backroads at: 1-800-462-2848 or try their web site at: www.backroads.com.

75. Have your employees sit in a circle. Each employee is asked to provide one sentence to a story. Ask for a volunteer to write down each sentence as the employee speaks it and read it back to everyone periodically. If the employees like the story they have created, then they can act it out. Many stories can be created in one sitting, and then the group can decide which to act out.

76. Surprise a deserving employee by filling his or her workstation with balloons.

77. On St. Patrick's day to encourage the luck of the Irish try this: encourage employees to wear green. Provide green mints throughout the day. Serve traditional Irish fare in the cafeteria. At noon, bring together the "Irish" lads and lassies for a contest to determine the "best dressed." Invite an Irish folk dance troupe to entertain in exchange for a monetary contribution to their organization.

78. A call center manager threw a "Slumber Party Saturday." Everyone showed up in pajamas, robes, and slippers for the late shift. Just be sure to outline the rules to avoid someone using bad judgement in selecting their sleepwear for the office.

79. Ask you employees to write wild and crazy personal mission statements—anything goes as long as it's not offensive. Everyone shares their statements at the end of a staff meeting.

Chapter 7 - Community Spirit

"Joy can be real only if people look upon their life as a service and have a definite object in life outside themselves and their personal happiness."

—Leo Tolstoy

Helping one's fellow human beings brings tremendous fulfillment and a sense of contribution to both individuals and organizations alike. By participating in charitable and community events, people help other people make their dreams come true. Whether it's your department who gives up their Saturday to help build a house for the Habitat for Humanity or an organization sponsoring athletes to compete in the Special Olympics, there are many ways to volunteer or donate time, money, and individual efforts.

Community spirit can also happen within your own organization. You'll find an example in this chapter where co-workers pooled their sick leave and gave it to an ill employee whose sick leave was running out.

Do whatever you can to encourage your employees to participate in charitable and community events. Let them use designated office time to organize their efforts for a specific project. Acknowledge their good deeds with plaques, special notices in the company newsletter, or a one-page ad in the community newspaper.

Volunteering is a year-round endeavor where everybody wins. Don't let your employees' efforts go unnoticed. You'll see plenty of ideas below on how your organization and employees can contribute to the future of your community and the people it serves.

1. Employees in an Atlanta-based company started the year by getting involved with the Foundation for Hospital Art. The organization sponsors "paintfests" that engage hundreds of participants who paint and provide artwork to brighten the lives of hospital patients. Foundation paintings hang in more than 500 hospitals in 165 countries. For more information: www.hospitalart.org or 770-645-1717.

2. Employees of one company collected new and used books for the Children's Restoration Network's Recycled Book Shop. The Book Shop is a nonprofit organization that supports children living in shelters and group homes in metro Atlanta. For information try: www.childrcn.org or 770-649-7117.

3. One compnay held an "Every Cents Counts" campaign. Coin banks were place thoughout the building. Money collected during the month of December went to pay past-due-rent or utility bills or buy food for low income seniors.

44

Community Spirit continued…

4. Gaylord Nelson, a U.S. Senator from Wisconsin, founded Earth Day on April 22 in 1970. Get your employees involved in hands-on volunteerism. Hold a park, stream or lake cleanup. Raise consciousness regarding environmental issues such as global warming, ozone layer, pollution, and extinction. For more information, contact their web site at: www.earthday.net.

5. In one community, the employees held fundraisers to raise money so they could buy and donate a horse to their local police department that uses it for patrolling at the mall on weekends and during special events. Thereafter, every year, the employees throw a birthday party for the horse.

6. Employee volunteers raised money toward the purchase of a 3-acre Natural Bear Habitat for a Wildlife Rehab Sanctuary. The rehab center takes orphaned and injured indigenous animals for rehabilitation and release back into the wild.

7. Hold a contest for the gardeners among your employees to see who can grow the largest tomato, cucumber, squash, watermelon, or other summer vegetables. Donate money to a charity of the employee's choice based upon a premium price for each pound the winning vegetables weigh in various categories.

8. At one company, employees collected prom dresses to give to low-income teenagers for upcoming proms. They also helped sponsor an alcohol/drug-free post-prom party. The employees had as much fun as the teens.

9. When a co-worker was being treated with chemotherapy and had used up his sick leave, fellow workers pooled their sick leave and gave it to him so that he wouldn't be without income during his recovery.

10. One compnay held a "bid for a date with a bachelor firefighter." All proceeds went to the community's Burn Foundation.

11. Sponsor an annual "Charity Day." Employees volunteer to work on a Saturday for a charity of their choice and donate their pay for the day to the charity. The company matches their contribution dollar for dollar.

12. Underwrite a special exhibit to a museum in exchange for free tickets for your employees to see the exhibit.

13. Give employees one-half day off with pay to shop for those who can't. One company begins the holiday season by buying gifts for a family whose name was pulled from the Salvation Army Christmas tree at the local mall.

14. Employees of one company raise money to equip K-9 Officers. Equipment includes a cooling vest, special leashes for the dogs, protective footwear, and an overdose kit.

45

Community Spirit continued...

15. Employees collect and donate "gently worn" clothing to a clothing bank for people who need proper interview and work attire.

16. Boo! At the Zoo. A zoo-wide scavenger hunt is the highlight of one organization's fund-raiser Halloween event for its employees. Employees purchase tickets and money is donated to children's charities in the community.

17. When an employee needed a kidney transplant, co-workers rallied around him and held a silent auction. Items were donated by local businesses as well as employees. Pictures of the items were placed on the company Intranet. Employees submitted bids via e-mail. On the deadline date, top bidders were notified and merchandise and cash was exchanged. Proceeds were given to the transplant patient to help offset expenses not covered by health insurance.

18. A group of animal lovers sponsored a community drive to collect used blankets and bath towels that they donated to their local animal shelter.

19. As a holiday gift to their local police department, employees raised and donated money to purchase several heavy-duty bulletproof vests at a cost of $1,200 each.

20. Adult trick-or-treaters of one company participated in "Sight Night," the Lion's Club/LensCrafters program that collects used eyeglasses for people in developing countries. They collected donations at the company and knocked on doors on October 31 in their neighborhoods.

21. In one company, a team of employees is responsible for researching charitable foundations and making recommendations. Then the entire employee population votes on which ones they want to support that year.

22. If your employees collect toys and clothing for under privileged children, hold a "gift wrapping" contest. Award prizes in different categories.

23. Hold a "Diaperama." Employees of one company collected diapers (size infant through 5) and wet wipes for A Beacon of Hope Women's Center.

24. Employees collected and donated money to The Elephant Sanctuary, a refuge for old, injured, and sick elephants from American zoos and circuses. It's located in Hohenwald, Tennessee. Two dollars will pay for a 6-by-12 foot space, big enough for an elephant to stand in. For more information visit: www.elephants.com.

25. Give employees company time to fill Christmas stockings. Deliver one to every child in a homeless shelter or sell them via a company-wide auction with proceeds going to charity.

Community Spirit continued...

26. Employees of a software company organized a non-competitive all-night continuous *Relay for Life* walk to raise money for cancer research. Families, friends, and businesses in the area sponsored employees. People walked in teams of up to 15 people around a high school track. Teams camped around the track and were entertained by line dancers, live bands, and professional masseurs while waiting their turn to relay. Awards were given for the *Best Decorated Campsite* and *Best Team Spirit.* Each team member paid a registration fee of $10 and was challenged to raise a minimum of $100. The money went to support the American Cancer Society's programs of research, cancer control, and patient services. For more information about *Relay for Life* call the American Cancer Society in your community.

27. To pay tribute to those who lost their lives in the cause of liberty, employees of one company planted a Liberty Garden using red, white, and blue flowers or foliage to creatively reflect the theme of patriotism.

28. One employer community supports its Boy Scouts who collect food for their county's Harvest Food Bank that serves 600 food pantries and meal programs. Employers provide trucks, storage space, workers to sort and bag food, etc. Over the past 14 years, the Scouts have collected over 1.8 million pounds of food.

29. Several companies in one community adopted an overseas Navy squadron for the holiday season. Employees collected donations including movies, CDs, books, magazines, nonperishable food and more.

30. A hair salon owner takes her employees to an elementary school in an impoverished neighborhood once a month and provides free haircuts for the children.

31. A fundraiser called *Fairy Tale Tea Friends* included puppet shows, costumed fairy tale characters, storytelling, face painting and a tea party. Employee volunteers of a local company presented this to the community.

32. Help feed the hungry by joining a "Plant a Row For The Hungry" campaign. The gardeners among your employees volunteer to plant extra vegetables (one row or more) and donate the produce to a local program that could benefit from the food.

33. Employees of several companies held a pizza fundraiser to raise money for the area's neediest public schools. Teachers were spending almost $500 of their own money for classroom supplies every year. Thanks to many generous people, they can now help themselves to free supplies at the local school supply store.

Community Spirit continued...

34. Employees in one company volunteer to tutor children for whom English is their second language. They tutor on their own time but are honored for their efforts every year at a banquet sponsored by the company. They work closely with an "after school learning center." The employees have found it to be extremely rewarding and the kids enjoy the one-on-one adult relationships which many of them don't have at home.

35. Turtle races are sponsored by a company for their community to raise money for their county's zoo. Events include races for land and sea turtles. The winning turtle is crowned "Queen or King Turtle" and takes a victory lap as the crowds cheer. Entry fees as well as an admission fee are charged.

36. Hold a "Way Out West Oktoberfest" with traditional German fare, from bratwurst and sauerkraut to dumplings, strudel and beer as does one company in San Diego. Employees are invited to participate by purchasing tickets for $5 per person. They may bring immediate family members. Money collected is donated to charity.

37. Employee's children participate in a "two for one" gift exchange. Children bring two toys when they attend the company holiday party. They leave both toys while picking out a new one to take home. The overflow toys are donated to Toys for Tots.

38. One company held a *Homage to Heroes* luncheon to honor the "heroes" of their local fire, police, and emergency medical service agencies.

39. Pay your employees for doing volunteer work. One day each quarter employees can work for a nonprofit agency of his or her choice and be paid by for their time.

40. Donate money to The Smile Train as employees of one company did. Local surgeons in developing countries provide life-changing free cleft palate surgery. Call them at: 1-877-KID-SMILE or check out their web site at: www.smiletrain.org.

41. Employees of one company collected and donated 250 teddy bears to their local police department's youth squad. Police use them during investigations at homes, police athletic leagues, hospitals, shelters, police precincts, and the Department of Family and Children Services. The bears help in getting upset children to relax and talk to authorities.

Other Books and CDs by Carol

366 MORE Surefire Ways to Let Your Employees Know They Count, InSync Press, 2002.

Employee loyalty a thing of the past? Maybe not. Competition is intense for recruiting good people. You've worked hard to get them in the door. Keeping them employed with you as happy, productive, and loyal workers is what this book is all about. It's a sequel to her first book on this subject and it leads the way with *more* surefire ways for letting your employees know they're appreciated. In Carol's newest book, she offers managers and supervisors, team leaders, and business owners dozens of concrete, creative and sometimes zany ideas for recognizing, rewarding and retaining employees. Think outside the usual work decorum box. Think fun on the job without spending a lot of money.

How to Compete in the War for Talent—A Guide to Hiring the Best, DC Press, 2001.

Are you tired of fighting for good people? Is your team's performance a casualty of high turnover? Is it possible you're not experiencing a shortage of personnel but a shortage of skills? If you're open to new ways of recruiting talent for your organization this book is a must-read. Leaders at all levels can benefit from the practical wisdom compiled in this book.

Retain or Retrain: How to Keep the Good Ones from Leaving, Co-author, InSync Press, 2001.

Seven experts from varying experiential backgrounds have pulled together to write this book of answers to the ever-growing problem of employee turnover. How can a company regardless of its size keep good people from leaving for greener pastures? This book offers practical solutions for preventing your employees from slipping through your fingers. It provides a variety of approaches to help managers keep their talent base, even in a tight job market.

366 Surefire Ways to Let Your Employees Know They Count, InSync Press, 2000.

Sometimes employees need a little extra incentive to encourage them to stick with you. People who enjoy what they do and who they work with become more valuable to the organization. They're usually happier as well. It's important for managers and business owners to encourage employees to reach their potential. Compensation isn't the only motivator. This book contains dozens of incentive ideas—many of them are quite simple, but are often overlooked.

450 Low-Cost/No-Cost Strategies for recognizing, rewarding & retaining good people, Revised 2002.

This is the original breakthrough book on a hot topic! It contains hundreds of low-cost/no-cost ideas for rewarding and recognizing good performance as well as building fun into your organization. Many of the suggestions have been used before; others are new but are currently being successfully implemented in organizations of all kinds throughout North America. You can apply the ideas in this book immediately and with confidence.

Other Books and CDs by Carol

Job Hunting in the 21st Century—Exploding the Myths, Exploring the Realities, St. Lucie Press, 1999.

Misconceptions about the job-hunting process have sabotaged the attempts of many job seekers. This book brings the reader up-to-date on the realities of understanding and mastering the job search process. It provides concepts that are easy to apply and presents the most current information on how to find a job in today's job market. It examines the most common job-hunting myths and offers solutions for avoiding the pitfalls associated with each.

Hiring Top Performers—350 Great Interview Questions For People Who Need People, Revised 2002.

Ideal for businesses of all sizes, in all industries, this book offers 350 sample interview questions in eight categories to help you get the information needed to make good hiring decisions. It's written in clear language and offers practical guidance to hiring managers at all levels.

The High Cost of Low Morale ...and what to do about it, St. Lucie Press, 1996.

Morale is an elusive quality. It's a feeling that's created within every employee. When morale is high, it's worth its weight in gold. This book contains over 125 interviews with top business leaders that reveal inside tips for keeping employees motivated to do their best. It offers time-tested advice to help keep your team energized and on track.

20 Costly Hiring Mistakes and How to Avoid Them – 47 minute CD – 2002

With the average cost of a bad hiring decision climbing to a whopping 30% of the first year's potential earnings, your choices are more important than ever before. In a live interview, get tips from a pro on how to avoid the astronomical costs associated with hiring the wrong person for the job.

How to Conduct "Win-Win" Performance Evaluations – 75 minute CD – 2002

Impact your bottom line immediately by learning how to stop the uncertainty and anxiety of evaluating employee performance. Learn how to set measurable goals and focus on future profitability. Listen to this CD and walk away knowing how to use performance evaluation as a motivational tool.

Low-Cost/No-Cost Strategies for Motivating Your Employees – 69 minute CD – 2002

It's a known fact that motivated, well-directed employees produce satisfied, loyal customers. This Teleseminar begins with the premise that "motivation is an inside job." Although we can't get inside the heads of our employees we can create a motivating environment where people want to work, learn, achieve, and make a difference. On this popular CD, Carol shares dozens of time-tested, low-cost/no-cost strategies for creating a motivating place to work.

A Sample of Carol's Seminars

Enhancing Working Relationships: This seminar is designed for anyone who manages, supervises or leads employees who are at times difficult and challenging.

Winning Back Morale in Emotional Times: This seminar is about morale—how to keep what you already have and how to regain what you've lost.

How to Give Critical Feedback and Make Your Employees Love You For It!: Learn how to convert criticism in your business from a painful confrontation into a successful experience for everyone!

Auditioning for High Morale—How to Hire a Motivated Workforce: Learn how to be a discriminating "buyer" and hire self-motivated people the first time around.

How to Keep the People Who Keep You in Business: This seminar examines key trends, outlines winning strategies, and offers helpful ideas for keeping the people who keep you in business.

Making Your Workplace Team-Productive and Hassle-Free: For managers and supervisors who want to make a difference.

Building and Leading a High-Performance Team: Find out how to build a balanced team with players who are willing to go the extra mile.

15 Team-Management Habits of Highly Successful Owners and Managers: Information for this seminar is culled from extensive interviews with business owners and managers as well as their staffs.

Power Hiring: How to Implement a High-Impact Recruiting Strategy: Learn how to turn a job interview into a sound and defensible hiring decision.

How to Reduce Turnover and Boost Your Bottom Line!: In this seminar we're throwing a goodbye party to employee turnover!

Color Outside the Lines: Creative Strategies for Selecting & Keeping Winning Employees for Your Business: Walk away with tips and techniques for your most pressing hiring and retention challenges.

The High Cost of Low Morale ...and what to do about it: Proven strategies that work regardless of the type of business, employees' positions, or levels of sophistication, pay status, or seniority.

Leadership in a Changing Environment: This seminar offers practical solutions for surviving tough times that can be put to use immediately.

How to be a Leader That Everyone Wants to Work For: Learn how new opportunities can lead to overcoming challenges, enduring fallout, and emerging as a highly valued leader.

51